Be an Anticipator!

Cindy Arledge

CUR$E
OF INHERITANCE

HOW TO PROTECT YOUR FAMILY
FROM BEING BROKE, BITTER AND BLAMING YOU

Cindy Arledge

CUR$E
OF INHERITANCE

**HOW TO PROTECT YOUR FAMILY
FROM BEING BROKE, BITTER AND BLAMING YOU**

Cindy Arledge

Praise for Cindy Arledge and
CUR$E OF INHERITANCE

"I speak from experience when I counsel you to read and take to heart what you learn from this book. Ignorance is not bliss when it comes to inheritance. Adopting this information will not only change your life, it will improve the entire dynamic of your family."

—Bobbi Schwartz, Founder and CEO of
Be Iconic Style

"My husband and I have been real estate investors for more than 20 years. We are all too familiar with the Cur$e of Inheritance. We've seen countless homes over the years owned by heirs of unplanned estates that end up in foreclosure or taken by the county for property taxes. The family ends up with broken relationships and no proceeds from what is often the most valuable portion of their loved one's estate. Over and over again they say, 'I never expected this from my siblings.'"

—Toni D. Lott, HomeVestors,
We Buy Ugly Houses™ Franchisee

"It isn't often we get simple advice for complex problems, but Cindy Arledge has managed to succinctly navigate the complexities of inheritance. Whether you are the beneficiary of an inheritance or the benefactor, this is a must read for the entire family. She writes from the heart and mind, and is straight forward and full of empirical data."

—Kathy Miner, Award-winning 5-Star Realtor

Praise for
My Camino, My Life

"Cindy's humorous and inspiring story is a great read for anyone considering walking the Camino or seeking more out of life."

—John P. Strelecky, #1 best-selling author of
The Why Cafe

"Cindy Arledge is a spirited & heart-centered entrepreneur. Her journey across the Camino is an inspiration. I admire her ability to turn grief into power. She can help you live with purpose, prosperity and joy."

—Mastin Kipp, best-selling author of
Daily Love: Growing into Grace

"I didn't know I needed the lessons, but they leapt from the pages and into my soul! I found myself smiling throughout the tale, and I could imagine myself right there with her. Cindy's insight and thoughts spoke to my heart and purpose."

—Brenna Smith, Founder and CEO
SheNOW, LLC

CUR$E OF INHERITANCE
Copyright © 2016 by Cindy Arledge
Published by: Legacy Inheritance Partners, Ltd
All Rights Reserved

5100 Eldorado Parkway, Suite 102-703
McKinney, TX 75070

Cover design by Brian Moreland
Interior layout design by Brian Moreland
Illustrations by Lisa Rothstein

ISBN 978-0-9826953-3-3

Disclaimer

This book is sold with the understanding that the publisher and author are not engaged in rendering legal, accounting or other professional services. Anyone planning to take action in any of the areas mentioned in this book should seek legal and expert assistance of trusted and competent professionals.

With the exception of the author's personal experiences, any similarity to actual people or places is coincidental. Names and places have been altered to protect confidentiality, and many stories are a compilation of actual experiences known to the author. Examples of Avoiders, Acceptors and Anticipators are the author's opinion only and are based on known facts concerning status of will and behavior of family members after death.

Every effort has been made to make this book as complete and accurate as possible. However, there may be mistakes both typographical and in content. Therefore, this text should be used only as a general guide.

The purpose of this book is to educate, empower, and inspire action. The author and Legacy Inheritance Partners, Ltd shall have neither liability nor responsibility to any person or entity with respect to any loss or damage caused or alleged to be caused directly or indirectly by the information contained in this book. Upon receipt of purchase, if you do not wish to be bound by the above, you may return this book to the publisher for a full refund.

Acknowledgements

To Gerald, my dear husband, thank you for your continuous support. You are the compass that guides me through my chaos.

To Tiffany, my daughter, business partner and friend. Your efforts to organize my office, thoughts and systems are greatly appreciated.

My children and grandchildren, you are the bridge to our future. I pray you take the best I have to offer, and ignore the rest.

To our Legacy Family members, those unborn generations, I pray the legacy we are building stands the test of time.

To Lisa Rothstein, thank you for bringing this book to life with your illustrations.

To Brian Moreland, the book genius who brings everything together.

To Susan Arledge and Tim Went, your support is greatly appreciated.

Chris and Pam Hendrickson, Mike Koenigs, Ed Rush, thank you for sharing your wisdom and building such supportive communities.

To my friends who know me best and continue to love me as I am: Kim Wallace, Thom Ricks, Jodi Stauffer, Brenna Jue, Dennis De Naut, Russ Riddle, Mike Matthews, my Artist Way Tribe and the CPSisters. Because of your continued belief and support, I stayed the course.

To my parents,
E. K. "Sandy" and Janice Arledge.
In honor of your hard work and sacrifice,
I changed myself first and by example, the family.
Together, we may better our country,
And perhaps change the world.

Table of Contents

Why I Wrote This Book

Becoming an orphan at any age is traumatic. Losing a parent you see occasionally is hard. But losing a parent that is part of your everyday life is even harder. The greater your daily life is impacted, the greater your grief will be. At the age of 46, I became an orphan and my life was turned upside down and inside out. It made me question everything I thought I knew about myself and life.

I am the only daughter and youngest child of E.K. "Sandy" and Janice Arledge. Dad passed away on March 4, 2005, the day after his 76th birthday. Exactly eight months later, at the age of 75, my mom passed away on November 4th. What followed, in distributing their estate, can only be described as horrific. My passion to help you and your family was born from the pain I experienced after my parents' deaths.

Before they passed, I foolishly believed I was mentally and emotionally prepared for life as an orphan. It began when I was 11 years old. Dad was only 40 when he survived his first bypass heart surgery. He bounced back to live through another bypass, six heart attacks, back surgery and prostate cancer. When he was diagnosed with lung cancer, even though the odds were against him, I held out hope that he would beat it. After all, his track record was immaculate. But when he fell and broke his hip in the midst of his cancer treatments, I knew he was done. A few weeks later he passed away.

Over several decades, I watched my mom slowly disappear. Scleroderma whittled her body away, and Alzheimers stole her mind.

Despite my parents' many health issues, I don't remember them as being sick. My memories reside in their enjoyment of travel, adventure and love of life.

After they were gone, I quickly discovered how unprepared I was to live life without them. I wasn't alone. My siblings, struggling with their own issues, and I found ourselves in an abyss of broken relationships that left me confused, lost and heart broken. Our experience was neither uncommon, nor new.

*"You don't really know someone
until you share an inheritance with them."*

--Paraphrasing Johann Kaspar Lavater,
a German Theologian born in 1741

Because we were unprepared, and our ability to communicate and trust each other was non-existent, we unleashed a dark monster I now know as the *Cur$e of Inheritance.*

The birth of my grandchildren made me realize that it was time to prepare my children to receive their inheritance. Unless something changed, they were destined to experience the same pain and heartache that I felt after my parents passed away.

Like others who have come before me, my mess has become my message. While I was dealing with my inheritance issues, I asked questions. New ones. I was tenacious in my search for answers because grandchildren change everything. I didn't want them to suffer as I did, and I don't want you or your family to suffer either.

During my research on inheritance and prosperity, I discovered a small group of families who successfully transfer wealth generation after generation. They are known as Legacy Families. Together, with my husband and children, we are implementing the secrets of these families to create our own **Legacy Family**.

If you aren't familiar with this term yet, you might be curious to know what it means. After reading this book, not only will you be familiar with a Legacy Family, I hope you will be inspired to build your own Legacy Family and share this revolutionary idea with your friends and family.

Currently, relationships with my siblings, in-laws, nieces and nephews range from vastly improved to stubbornly broken. By healing myself first, then sharing my story, I come from a place of gratitude for all that has happened. I have no need or desire to make anyone a villain. We were all victims.

As painful as the family fallout was, I have received many gifts. I learned I can love someone who continues to hate me. I learned how to create healthy boundaries in toxic relationships. And, I learned how to love and support someone without attaching strings.

It's time to revolutionize the estate planning

industry. In this book, I discuss the real problem, explain what the Cur$e of Inheritance is and the issues that are affecting people who are unprepared. Then I offer solutions so you can begin to prepare and protect your family. Legacy planning has the potential to prevent 85% of wealth transfer failures.

You will find many valuable resources offered throughout this book. When you sign up for one at our website, you will receive access to them all.

**Find resources to build your
Legacy Family Plan at:
www.LegacyFamilyRevolution.com**

Why You Should Read This Book ...

What you don't know can and will hurt you and your family. Odds are, you or someone you know has experienced a broken relationship after receiving an inheritance. From sentimental "stuff" to significantly valuable assets, battles can erupt without warning. It is so common and widespread to see families destroyed after an inheritance that it is accepted as normal.

Lottery winners, notorious for losing their winnings, have a better chance of retaining their wealth than inheritors, and lottery winners' odds are terrible. According to the National Endowment for Financial Freedom, 70% of lottery winners actually end up broke in a few years.

Sadly, the odds of heirs retaining their wealth are even less. Worldwide, throughout history, 75-90% of wealth transfers fail within three generations. This is called "shirtsleeves to shirtsleeves" in the United States, "clogs to clogs" in Ireland, and "rice paddies to rice paddies" in Japan.

What is going on? How can a failure rate of—let's keep it simple and say 85%—remain unchallenged?

While many grumble and shake their heads, the sad truth is that society has accepted failed inheritances as normal. Lack of understanding the real issue, the taboo topics of death and money, and no viable solution all contribute to the continued proliferation of broken families.

It doesn't have to be this way. My goal in writing this book is to expose the real cause for the Cur$e of Inheritance, break down conversation barriers about death and money and introduce you to a powerful solution. I want to educate and inspire you to protect your family so they won't be **broke, bitter and blaming you**. You deserve better and so do they.

I know this message isn't easy to digest. Conversations about death ranks right beside taxes, sex, money and politics. They are taboo topics that polite society avoids. Impolite society, too. Death makes us uncomfortable. In our discomfort, we avoid it until we can't avoid it any longer. When a crisis occurs, be it accident or diagnosis, the ensuing chaos reaffirms our discomfort with the topic. Some superstitious folks believe the act of preparing for death will actually cause it to happen sooner.

This book is the start of a Revolution! What you don't know can destroy your family. I am passionate about spreading this information to protect you and your loved ones. I have deliberately kept it short and easy to read so that it will be a quick read. There are times the content may trigger emotions, but please keep reading. After you finish this book you'll be inspired to create your own Legacy Family Plan.

Please let me know how it's going and how I can support you on your journey. My email address is info@legacyfamilyrevolution.com. I would very much like to hear from you about what you're doing with the ideas in this book.

All the best,

Cindy Arledge

Why Now?

This is a historic moment in time in our nation. The United States population is about to experience the largest wealth transfer that has ever occurred. According to *InvestmentNews*, conservatively, over $30 trillion dollars of wealth will transfer in the next 30 years. The number of millionaires is increasing. Baby boomers are setting the stage for this epic event, not only with the money they saved, but with inherited gains from their parents.

Through the eyes of someone who has lived through the Cur$e, our nation is facing a tragedy of epic proportions that most people have yet to recognize.

The American family is clueless to the greatest threat it has ever faced: The Cur$e of Inheritance.

It's time to fix this broken system. You must educate yourself and become part of the solution. In the courtroom, ignorance is not a justifiable defense. But in estate planning, I believe ignorance plays a significant role in wealth transfer failures.

Lacking information is nothing to be ashamed of. Having the information and ignoring it is another matter. I was greatly impacted by a high school poster that read, "If you aren't part of the solution, you are part of the problem."

Time is of the essence.
Be a part of the solution,
The legacy family revolution.

My Story

Having worked for my parents the majority of my life, managing their money wasn't new for me. At 13, I was hired as Mom's assistant bookkeeper for our wholesale car business. By 17, I was promoted to the trucking company, and responsible for keeping our portable parking lots (18-wheeler car haulers) legal in 21 states. Mind you, this was before the deregulation of the trucking industry. When tax laws changed, Dad's business model of leasing cars to major car rental companies was no longer viable, and a second bypass surgery convinced him to retire.

His prior rental car customers now needed locations to sell their cars, and they asked Dad for help. He was feeling better, bored with retirement and loved making deals. The rental car companies didn't want to own real estate, so Dad became their landlord with locations across Texas, and even one in Tennessee.

Between deals, Mom and Dad roamed the countryside in their motorhome for months at a time. While they were gone, I kept the real estate business going. When Dad purchased new properties, I was right by his side. Looking back, I realize he provided me with a lifetime of business mentorship and family leadership. But he made a serious mistake that caused problems after his death. He failed to tell my siblings of his plan, and he gave up on training and mentoring them.

A few years before Dad died, Gerald, my third husband, and I started our own business and I was no longer available to help Dad fulltime. He hired an assistant to replace me, and when Mom and Dad traveled, I continued to sign checks and help with any issues that arose.

Looking back, I realize I never saw their stuff as ever belonging to me. In the two years between their deaths and the distribution of their estate, I was uncomfortable anticipating my inheritance. I was confused, so I began reading books on inheritance, money, prosperity and consciousness. I wanted to honor my parents and be able to pass down the wealth they had built to future generations. I wanted their hard work and sacrifice to matter, to make the world a better place.

The problem was, I didn't know how to honor them and I was still reeling from the broken relationships with my brothers and their families. In the midst of my confusion, the following poem put me on the right path.

In the Crypts of Westminster Abbey, an Epitaph from the Tomb of an Anglican Bishop (AD 1100):

When I was young and free and my imagination had no limits, I dreamed of changing the world. As I grew older and wiser, I discovered the world would not change, so I shortened my sights somewhat and decided to change only my country.

But it, too, seemed immovable.

As I grew into my twilight years, in one last desperate attempt, I settled for changing only my family, those closest to me, but alas, they would have none of it.

And now, as I lie on my deathbed, I suddenly realize: If I had only changed myself first, then by example I would have changed my family.

From their inspiration and encouragement, I would then have been able to better my country and who knows, I may have changed the world.

Because of the family business, my life was intertwined with my parents' lives. I also spent more time with them because I was their only daughter, and the baby of the family. In the wake of their absence, I had to redefine myself, and in some ways, discover who I was for the first time. Mentally, physically and spiritually, I was aching. I was in the depths of the "dark night of the soul."

This poem profoundly impacted me because it provided me with clear direction. I wanted to change the world and honor my parents, and the place to start was by changing myself.

To change myself I studied universal laws and ancient wisdom from several sources. From my research, I melded a set of ideas, beliefs, attitudes, practices and tools into a formula for living that I called GRIPP Life™. GRIPP is an acronym for Gratefully, Responsibly, Intentionally Pursuing Purpose. Using the GRIPP Life™ Formula, I was able to rebuild my life. It enabled me to feel prosperous despite the several million dollars of debt I borrowed to settle my parents' estate right BEFORE the 2008 market crash. It also helped me remain centered when my brother Richard was wrongfully convicted of conspiracy and sentenced to a federal prison. He refused to plead guilty and continues to maintain his innocence and has served 3 years of a 16-year sentence for a victimless crime. Victimless, according to the government report. The GRIPP Life™ Formula has helped me accept his situation without judgment or feeling like a victim to the injustice he is enduring.

Despite these successes, I wanted to be 100% sure the formula worked before sharing it with others. I decided to conduct one more experiment. I walked the Camino de Santiago, an ancient 500-mile pilgrimage across Spain over a period of 37 days. When I returned, I wrote my first book, *My Camino, My Life: A Sole to Soul Connection.* In the writing process, I became a witness to my own healing and discovered, instead of sharing the GRIPP Life™ Formula, it was time to create my Legacy Family and warn others of the Cur$e of Inheritance.

**Warning:
what you are about
to learn
may shock you.**

The Cause of the Problem

Most people think money
is the problem.
They are wrong.

AVOIDING DEATH IS THE PROBLEM!

Death makes us uncomfortable. We act as though we aren't going to die.

We do our best to avoid thinking about it, talking about it, or preparing for it.

55%
of the adult population
doesn't even have a will.

And for those who have a will, the vast majority remain uncomfortable with the idea of dying and do the minimum to prepare.

In other words . . . even when we legally prepare for death, we aren't comfortable facing our mortality.

Isn't it interesting that we resist, avoid and ignore the **one thing** that life guarantees?

**We don't know
when it will happen,
but at some point,
we are all going to die.**

**SPOILER ALERT:
You don't have to be old to die.**

Like an ostrich with its head
in the sand, refusing to get
a will won't prevent
your need for one.

**Refusing to prepare for death
increases your family's
suffering.**

COMPOUNDING THIS PROBLEM,
money amplifies.

Money is amoral. It is neither good nor bad. It only makes you more of what you are.

More money amplifies your current relationship with it.

If you're generous, more money makes you more generous.

If you're greedy, more money makes you greedier. If you're confused, like I was, more money makes you more confused.

COMPLICATING THIS PROBLEM...
unearned wealth is cursed.

Things received without
effort come with
a spiritual attachment.
You may know it as
"a free lunch."

The Kabbalists call it
"the Bread of Shame."

The Bread of Shame
is a little known, but powerful
force.

Just ask any lottery winner!

Inheritance is an insidious form of the Bread of Shame.

Think about it for a moment. Someone had to die first. **(Presumably, a loved one.)**

Without preparation, unearned wealth received after a loved one's death feels dirty.

This is called: The **Cur$e** of Inheritance.

The **Cur$e** of Inheritance is an ugly monster of jealousy, fear and selfishness that crushes families, eats money and destroys lives.

The **Cur$e** of Inheritance is born in an environment of loss and grief, by unprepared heirs who feel entitled to unearned wealth, and tragically forget to see each other as human beings.

The Effect
of the Problem

85%
of wealth transfers fail.

By fail, I mean breakdown
of the family unit, loss of
financial assets, and emotional
upheaval for family members.

Isn't it time to fix
this broken system?

Even more tragic,

the broken system

is accepted

as normal.

**Most people
don't understand that . . .**

Legacy and Inheritance
are **NOT** the same.

Legacy is seen through
the **giver's eyes**.

Inheritance is viewed through
the **eyes of the receivers**.

When givers fail to see how their gift will be seen through the receivers' eyes, they unwittingly unleash the Cur$e of Inheritance.

Giving money

to unprepared heirs

can ruin their lives.

The Solution
of the Problem

Have the courage to anticipate your death, prepare for it and educate and train your family for life after you are gone.

Ironically, taking this action

opens the door

to a fulfilling life!

Your action, or inaction,

will impact your family

for generations to come.

The Legacy Family Secret

During my research, I discovered a small group of families who successfully transfer wealth. These Legacy Families don't suffer from the three-generation cycle of shirtsleeves to shirtsleeves, in part from the support they receive from a little known industry called the "Home Office."

Each Home Office has different requirements, but most require a portfolio of 30 million dollars of investable assets. Top offices require 100 million dollars! But, if you're like me and you don't have 30 to 100 million dollars to invest, no worries. You don't have to be ultra-rich to create a Legacy Family. I'm not saying that you don't need some assets, and quite frankly the more the better. But not being super rich doesn't disqualify you from Legacy Family status.

You don't need a home office to be successful and you don't have to spend thousands of hours of research like I did. I've done the hard work for you. You do need courage to change your mindset about death and money, and the willingness to implement a proven plan that works.

What you won't be able to do is to forget the information in this book. You will be faced with a decision. Will you summon the courage to change yourself, to better your family?

What Makes a Legacy Family Successful?

Prepare yourself.

It's
not
about
the
money.

Legacy Families use a secret planning tool— The Legacy Family Plan.

The Legacy Family Plan provides for a systematic transfer of values and character, as well as the intentional development of competencies in the four capital accounts (Financial, Social, Intellectual and Human), by assisting family members to achieve their unique and highest potential.

You see, Legacy Families anticipate death. They not only plan for it, they provide training for the next generation, "the Rising Generation."

Legacy Family planning prepares heirs and builds communication and trust. It prevents the **Cur$e of Inheritance** from growing in the hearts of heirs.

Now It's Your Turn

Have the courage to answer the question "How can I help my heirs be successful with their inheritance?" Although you may never be comfortable facing your own mortality, now is the time to prepare for it, plan for it and discuss it. Empower your heirs by providing them with the education, knowledge and resources they will need after you are gone. Use the Legacy Family Planning toolkit to protect your family from being broke, bitter and blaming you!

In this book you will discover:

- What is a Will?
- The Legacy Family Estate Planning Pyramid (LFEPP)
- The Estate Planning Assessment Tool
- Your current position on the LFEPP and what it means for your family's future
- The critical, unavoidable first step
- The Basic Components of Legacy Family Planning
- The Basic Principles
- The Benefits of Legacy Family Planning

You are about to embark
on the most

**IMPORTANT JOURNEY
OF YOUR LIFE.**

Like any journey, you will hit
some rough spots. Remember
to avoid stopping while you're
trudging through the mud. When
the path gets sticky, keep going!
It's the only way to make it to the
top so you can enjoy the view.

What Is a Will?

This is a good time to get on the same page about a "will."

Just in case you skipped the disclaimer at the front of the book, I'm repeating myself here, because it is important that you know: this book **does not provide legal advice**. Please, contact your professional advisors for legal advice.

That being said, it is important that we are on the same page concerning the term "will." For the purposes of this book, "will" is a group of essential estate planning documents that, at a minimum, contain the following:

- Last Will and Testament

- Statutory Power of Attorney

- Power of Attorney for Health Care

- DNR-Do Not Resuscitate

Each family is different, your list of needed documents may be more extensive.

By the way, everyone **over 18 years old needs a will**. Sounds bizarre, but providing a will as a birthday gift for newly adult children exemplifies financial maturity.

Legacy Family Estate Planning Pyramid

The Legacy Family Estate Planning Pyramid (LFEPP) measures an individual's ability to prepare for death, which in turn, determines the family's position on the pyramid. The better prepared an individual is for death, the more favorable outcome can be expected for the family.

The LFEPP consists of two sides with three levels each.

The left side of the pyramid **measures your personal level of death prep-aration**. The three levels are *Avoider, Acceptor* and *Anticipator*.

The right side of the pyramid **predicts your family's future based on your preparation**. What you do matters and directly affects your family's future. The three levels are *Lost, Limited* and *Legacy*.

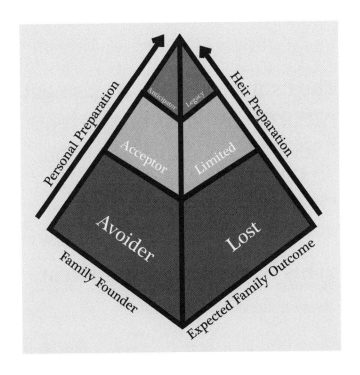

Start the journey now!

Complete the Assessment.

The Estate Planning Assessment Tool determines your current level of preparedness on the LFEPP.

This is not a pass or fail test.

Check the box next to the answer that best fits your current belief and attitude. Be honest with yourself. This is for your eyes only.

ESTATE PLANNING ASSESSMENT TOOL

*For a printable copy of this worksheet
and other companion tools, visit*
www.legacyfamilyrevolution.com

Estate Planning Assessment (EPA). Please don't overthink the questions. The 14 questions won't take long to complete. Trust your first response, even if none of the answers are perfect.

1. A plan to prepare my heirs:

A. _____ is not my problem
B. _____ my advisor's responsibility
C. ✓ my responsibility

2. My comfort level of discussing death is:

A. _____ not at all
B. ✓ I will, but prefer not to
C   _____ very comfortable

3. My estate planning status is:

A. ✓ someday I'll do it
B. _____ following traditional advice
C. _____ Legacy Family Plan in place

4. Has my family reviewed my Estate Plan?

A. ✓ No
B. _____ They are aware I have one, but haven't seen it
C. _____ Yes, the entire family has reviewed it

5. Control of my assets:

A. ____ belongs to me
B. __✓__ will transfer after I'm gone
C. ____ is controlled by a governance plan

6. At the end of my life, my financial plan is:

A. ____ to bounce my last check
B. __✓__ covered in my will
C. ____ detailed in my Legacy Family Plan

7. My focus is upon:

A. __✓__ today
B. ____ my current heirs, children
     and grandchildren
C. ____ unborn generations living 100 years
     from now

8. After my death, I hope my financial resources:

A. ____ are a non-issue; I'm planning on
     breaking even
B. __✓__ help my heirs, but I won't be around
     if they don't
C. ____ are invested according to my Legacy
     Family Plan

9. My financial goals are:

A. ____ to die at zero or bounce my last check
B. __✓__ based in hope that my heirs spend
     wisely
C. ____ known and already in use

10. How my heirs react to their inheritance is:
A. __✓__ not my problem
B. ____ my advisor's problem
C. ____ anticipated and planned for

11. My current advisors range from:
A. __✓__ none to Financial Planner
B. ____ Financial Planner, Attorney, CPA
C. ____ Financial Planner, Attorney, CPA,
       Mentors & Legacy Family Plan Advisor

12. The social impact of my finances is:
A. ____ not important
B. __✓__ important
C. ____ defined in a Stewardship Plan

13. In our family:
A. ____ most everyone gets along
B. __✓__ we enjoy holidays and special occasions
C. ____ we meet regularly for fun and
       family meetings

14. My family members:
A. ____ are on their own
B. ____ can count on me to bail them out if
       they get into trouble
C. __✓__ enjoy a self-sustaining lifestyle

CONGRATULATIONS, YOU'RE DONE!

Let's Calculate Your Score

The first step in calculating your score is to review your answers, count the number of times you answered each letter and then record the numbers below.

Total of # A Answers _____5_____

Total of # B Answers _____7_____

Total of # C Answers _____2_____

Total of all Responses _____14_____

Should total 14

The second step in calculating your score is to transfer the total for each response above and complete the multiplication for each level.

Calculate the Totals

___5___ X 1 = ___5___

Total # A Answers

___7___ X 2 = ___14___

Total # B Answers

___2___ X 3 = ___6___

Total # C Answers

Total points: = ___25___

Your Score

If you scored between 14 and 17, you are currently at the Avoider Level on the Legacy Family Estate Planning Pyramid.

Avoiders: 14 to 17

If you scored between 18 and 38, you are currently at the Acceptor Level on the Legacy Family Estate Planning Pyramid.

Acceptors: 18 to 38

If you scored between 39 and 42, you are currently at the Anticipator Level on the Legacy Family Estate Planning Pyramid.

Anticipators: 39 to 42

What does your score mean for your family?

Avoiders leave

Lost Families

Acceptors leave

Limited Families

Anticipators leave

Legacy Families

Caution:

*Regardless of your score,
if you don't have a valid will,
you are an Avoider.*

Avoiders and
the Lost Family

If you don't have a valid will,
your first step is to execute one.

Your Lost Family's future will be
determined by your state's law.

Without a valid will,
both you and your family are
in grave danger.

(pun intended)

Your action, or inaction, will affect your
family for generations to come. Please, for
the sake of your family, take this first step
and get a valid will.

Is this what you want for you and your family?

I presume your answer is "no" and that you love your family more than being an Avoider, and you now see that, unless you take action and start planning for your death, your loved ones will suffer after you are gone.

STOP!
NO NEED TO READ FURTHER
UNTIL YOU EXECUTE A VALID WILL.

Ultimately, we are only responsible for ourselves.

But if you have a significant other, why not make a date and get both wills done together?

Please take Action NOW!
There are no guarantees of tomorrow.

If you received this book from an advisor, please contact them. If obtaining a will is not their expertise, they will refer you to someone who can help.

If you are an Avoider with a valid will **you are to be congratulated!** While you have taken the most important first step in protecting your family, you have a ways to go.

**Remember, this is a journey.
It doesn't matter where you start.
It only matters where you end.**

I know this is not an easy topic to explore. I implore you to have the courage to keep reading. Avoid giving up on yourself or your family. If you find yourself getting angry, good! Anger is a compass, pointing you in the right direction.

The purpose of this book is to enlighten you to the reality your family faces and TAKE NECESSARY ACTIONS TO PROTECT YOUR LOVED ONES. I'm not sugar coating anything. It's time someone told the truth. Hopefully you will hear it.

**As you read forward,
please embrace the ideas
that resonate with you
and ignore the rest.**

Avoider's Mindset

As an Avoider, your focus is on today, yourself and control. Your financial plan is a gamble to die at zero, or bounce your last check. Preparing your heirs isn't your problem. Investing in social enterprises isn't important. You maintain control of your assets. Your advisors range from none to a Financial Advisor.

Family members are on their own. How they receive an inheritance, if there is one, is not your problem. If you completed an estate plan, you didn't share it with your family and you didn't talk about it. In the Avoider household, it's every man, woman and child for themselves.

Here's an unfortunate example of Avoiders being unprepared:

It was totally unexpected when she received the call that her 33-year-old husband was in the hospital for a heart attack he suffered while prepping for the New York Marathon. Their two young daughters suffered the most during his valiant six-week battle to live. Unfortunately, state law did not allow him to sign any documents in his medical condition, and he died intestate (without a valid will). This financially successful executive failed to protect his family for their greatest time of need. Accounts were frozen, and without her family's financial support during the years it took to probate his estate, they would have been homeless.

YOU ARE NOT ALONE.

The following people died without a will.
They were *Avoiders*.

Prince
Sonny Bono
John Denver
Howard Hughes
President Abraham Lincoln
Rita Hayworth
Martin Luther King, Jr.
Tupac Shakur

Without a will,
you remain an Avoider.
Avoiders leave Lost families.

Martin Luther King, Jr. Update:

48 years after his death, Martin Luther King, Jr's children settled their dispute out of court just days before their scheduled trial. This agreement ended their protracted dispute over the disposition of the slain civil rights leader's Nobel Peace Prize Medal and personal bible.

It's time to see what your family can expect: Avoiders create Lost Families.

For you . . .

The slightest economic hiccup, health issue or unexpected financial challenge could leave you short on finances and long on days. What is your backup plan for your shortfall?

Or the opposite could occur. You might be secretly saving a nice nest egg for your heirs and not telling them, thinking they will be pleasantly surprised. One thing I can say for sure, by not being open and upfront, they won't be prepared. Unearned wealth is cursed, especially when someone we love has to die for us to receive it.

For them . . .

Following your financial plan of bouncing your last check, if you ever needed help, your heirs probably won't be the ones to ask.

They don't know what you value, they don't know what is important for you, and they aren't a team.

Decision making by guessing is stressful and contentious, especially during chaotic times.

Surprise nest egg or not, your family is primed to unleash the Cur$e of Inheritance. It's not the **amount of money** that matters. It's the **unprepared heirs** who lack the ability to communicate and trust each other. Secretly planning to leave money to unprepared heirs can ruin their lives.

LOST FAMILIES SUFFER UNNECESSARY PAIN AND AGONY THAT ARE AVOIDABLE.

Is this what you want for you and your family?

I'm presuming your answer is "no" and that you love your family enough to get uncomfortable.

You are not in this alone. As you take the "next right step" approach, you will be guided along this journey.

Step One was to get a valid will. Did you do it yet, or did you skip that step and keep reading?

STOP!

Really, this book will still be here.
No need to read further if you
don't have a valid will.

If you did get your will done,

LET'S CELEBRATE!

It was a HUGE step to take.

It's time to take the next one.

Acceptors and the Limited Family

Acceptor's Mindset

As an Acceptor, your focus is on yourself and your current heirs. Control of your assets will transfer when you die. Making a positive social impact is important, but you haven't made a formal plan of the impact you desire to make. Your financial plan is covered in your will and you are counting on your advisors to prepare your heirs. Your advisors range from financial planner, CPA and attorney.

The family enjoys getting together on holidays and special occasions. Family members know that, when they get into a jam, you will bail them out, unless they ask one too many times. Then, they're on their own.

You will discuss death, but prefer not to. You follow traditional advice and have a will, but you haven't shared it with the family. You hope, after you die, their inheritance will help them, and you want them to spend it wisely. Whatever happens after you are gone, it's not your problem, your advisors will take care of it.

Here's an example of an Acceptor:

When Grandma died in her mid-eighties, her entire estate of $25,000 was earmarked for her daughter's son. He was the youngest grandson and she wanted to help with his college tuition. Unfortunately, Grandma failed to talk to her own son and now brother has accused sister of "getting it all" and they haven't spoken since. The family divide continues, as once loving siblings and cousins no longer see each other. Grandma discussing her plans with both of her children could have prevented this tragedy.

YOU ARE NOT ALONE.

The following famous and not so famous people were *Acceptors*:

E. K. "Sandy" and Janice Arledge
(the author's parents)
Reginald and Gloria Morgan Vanderbilt
(Gloria Vanderbilt's parents)
Michael Jackson
Andy Warhol
Leona Helmsley
Aristotle Onassis

It's not the amount of money that unleashes the Cur$e.

Money amplifies broken relationships that existed before the wealth transfer.

Staggering to consider, legal preparation isn't enough to protect your family.

Acceptors Leave Limited Families!

The outlook for the Limited Family is better than lost families, but remains a gamble. By preparing your will, you have provided your family with the legal tools they need to settle your estate. But failure to prepare your heirs means they are still subject to communication and trust issues that can destroy your family and waste precious resources.

The Danger for you:

Acceptors aren't comfortable talking about death. If you haven't clearly communicated your end-of-life desires with your **entire family at one time**, you are laying the foundation for misunderstanding and arguments. Reliance on paperwork without communication with your doctor increases the likelihood your medical wishes for your final care will not be honored.

The Danger for your family:

Your legal documents are a solid foundation for your family's protection. But they aren't enough to protect them from the Cur$e of Inheritance. The majority of wealth transfer failures happen due to a) communication issues and b) the gap in estate planning created by unprepared heirs who lack the ability to trust one another. Funds that could have gone to loved ones end up in the pockets of attorneys. It is not the attorney's fault, either. They provide services that consumers demand. Lawsuits are the effect of broken relationships. Heal the cause, broken relationships that create lawsuits in the future.

LIMITED FAMILIES OFTEN SUFFER UNNECESSARY PAIN AND AGONY THAT ARE AVOIDABLE.

My parents were Acceptors. They had an elaborate estate plan, but failed to fully follow their attorney's advice. Although trusts were set up, they were never funded. Despite assurances from his advisors, Dad was afraid he would lose control of his assets. More than once, Dad apologized for the tax liability he knew he had created. I never thought much about it when we discussed it. After all, it was his money, not mine. But, I wonder . . . had he known his fear would cost $1,833,385.12 in estate taxes, would he have made a different choice? My hand shook as I co-signed the IRS check, and I was grateful the check didn't bounce. Many families are unable to raise the necessary funds to pay their estate taxes and are forced to sell assets at discounted prices in a fire sale.

Dad changed his will after a disagreement with some family members. After her diagnosis of Alzheimers, Mom could not change her will. This made their two wills incompatible for the grandchildren's portions of their estates. My parents created the trusts so their grandchildren could receive monthly income from the real estate.

To overcome this incompatibility and settle their estate, the real estate from the grandchildren's trusts needed to be sold. In my desire to honor my parents' wishes, I violated my personal value system and borrowed 2.6 million dollars to purchase the real estate and settle the estate. The timing couldn't have been worse. We completed the purchase a few months before the Crash of 2008 crippled the U.S. economy. Ouch!

The big tax bill was a challenge, but Dad anticipated the taxes and pre-saved a large portion of them for us. The grandchildren's trust incompatibility wasn't easy, but we were able to resolve this issue as well. But Dad's decision to remove a few family members from his will unleashed the Cur$e of Inheritance. And once unleashed, it ravaged our family. It didn't matter that the family members that Dad kept in his will were not responsible for his decision, and that everyone inherited from Mom. The Cur$e is an ugly monster of jealousy, fear and selfishness that crushes families, eats money and destroys lives. There are no winners when the Cur$e is unleashed. Everyone is a victim.

Is this what you want for you and your family?

I'm presuming your answer is "no" and that you want **only the best for your family.**

KEEP READING!

This book provides the missing information you need to protect your family.

Please don't delay. There are no guarantees of tomorrow.

Anticipators and the Legacy Family

Anticipator's Mindset

Please keep in mind as you read this section that your goal is to prepare your heirs and build their trust and communication. Within each level on the Legacy Family Estate Planning Pyramid there is a spectrum. ***As a reminder, use what resonates, and ignore the rest.*** The mindset presented is the optimum position on the Anticipator spectrum, and depending on your needs, certain concepts may not apply to you.

As an Anticipator, your focus is setting a positive example, training your heirs and building a bridge to unborn generations to benefit from your life's contribution. Turning over a portion of your assets to your heirs while you are still alive, provides you the opportunity to train the next generation to follow in your footsteps. Social impact is important to you, and you have a plan. Your financial plan has been adopted by the rising generation while you are available to advise them. You have created a Board of Directors for your family that includes your financial planner, CPA, attorney, and other mentors.

The family conducts regular family meetings as well as enjoyable celebrations, vacations and get-togethers. Family members feel a strong sense of family unity with healthy boundaries.

You are not shy about discussing death; in fact you enjoy it, because it reminds you that "each day is a gift." Time is precious, and you appreciate the opportunity to use your gifts and talents to meet the world's needs to express your unique contribution. You are open to new ideas to prepare for your family's future. The rising generation has taken leadership of the family fortune, and you feel confident your Legacy Family Plan has provided a strong foundation to bridge the gap to future generations. The rising generation has accepted stewardship of financial resources and is actively engaged in preparing future generations.

YOU ARE NOT ALONE.

You are a part of a very elite group. Congratulations!

The following families and family-owned companies are *Anticipators*:

Kongo Gumi, Japan, 40th generation, construction, founded in 578

Barovier & Toso, Italy, 20th generation, glass making, founded in 1295

John Brooke & Sons, United Kingdom, 15th generation, fabric, founded in 1541

Zildjian Cymbal Co., United States, 14th generation, cymbals, founded in 1623

Nordstrom, United States, retailer, 4th generation, founded in 1901

Bill Bonner, author, CEO and founder of Agora, Inc.

Cindy Arledge and Gerald Fritz (the author and her husband)

Anticipators Leave Legacy Families!

The outlook for the Legacy Family is optimistic. You have demonstrated your courage to prepare for your death and spent considerable energy to prepare your family for life after you are gone to ensure their ability to flourish. Let's take a moment to review the Cur$e of Inheritance and how your ability to Anticipate can and can't protect them.

> *The Cur$e of Inheritance is an ugly monster of jealousy, fear and selfishness that crushes families, eats money and destroys lives.*
>
> *The Cur$e of Inheritance is born in an environment of loss and grief, by unprepared heirs who feel entitled to unearned wealth and forget to see each other as human beings.*

The environment of loss and grief can't be avoided. You will be missed and your family members will grieve. Deeply. However, by seeing your legacy through your heirs' eyes, you prepared them to accept stewardship of your financial resources.

Together, you built a foundation of gratitude, which is the antidote to entitlement. Implementing the Legacy Family Plan provided your heirs with the opportunity to resolve conflicts and overcome jealousy, fear and selfishness while you are here to help them.

The Benefit for you:

Based on current lifespans, odds are, you won't be around in 100 years to see the results of your effort. But, as an Anticipator, the joy is in the journey of building a Legacy Family. One of the greatest benefits of becoming an Anticipator is your ability to *own your life*. Every minute becomes precious; each day is a gift. Your life is your legacy, and as an Anticipator, your calendar and checkbook shift to match your values.

The Benefit for them:

In addition to the legal documents, your family members have spent time together preparing for a future without you. They have shared values, a family story and mission statement to guide them through challenging situations. They have an attitude of gratitude. There are no secrets. Childhood issues that typically surface when they become an orphan have had a chance to be aired—while you are alive. While everyone may not agree, they have been heard, and have a formalized internal grievance system to resolve their conflicts in a respectful manner. Once I discovered the Legacy Family concept, I knew it was the answer I was seeking for our blended family. Gerald brings one daughter to our family, and I bring two. All the girls are married, and my girls have two children each. At the time of this printing, we are a family of 12, with hopes of more grandchildren.

Gerald and I have been married almost 20 years. Between the two of us, we consider all three girls as our own and have set up our estate plan with each receiving an equal share. But how *we* feel, doesn't matter. It is the relationship between the girls, their husbands and eventually the grandchildren that counts.

By taking the best of the Legacy Family Planning research and combining it with the successfully tested theories of the GRIPP Life™ Formula, I created our Legacy Family Plan which I will be sharing in my next book, *The Legacy Family Way*.

Implementing our plan has been a fluid process. After the first meeting, where Gerald and I introduced the idea to the family, they took ownership of the process and have driven it forward. Gerald and I are the engine, but our rising generation's questions determine our path. When necessary, we schedule workshop days with our attorney, CPA and other advisors. But for the most part, our meetings have been half-day meetings, followed by time together just hanging out. Although it hasn't always been smooth, we are very pleased with the progress as we move through the process.

It is one of the greatest ironies of life. By having the courage to prepare for death, you enjoy living each day as a gift. Legacy Family Planning is the vehicle to protect your family's future after you are gone.

Before We Move On, Let's Recap

The Real Problem: Avoidance of death.

Compounding the problem: Money amplifies.

Complicating the Problem: Unearned wealth is cursed.

The Effect of the Problem: 85% of wealth transfers fail.

Our Wealth transfer system is broken and accepted as normal.

Legacy is seen through the giver's eyes. **Inheritance** is seen through the eyes of the receiver.

Leaving money to unprepared heirs can ruin their lives.

Your ability to prepare for death affects your family's future for generations to come.

Legacy Family Planning is the systematic transfer of values and character, as well as the intentional development of competencies in the four capital accounts (Financial, Social, Intellectual and Human), by assisting family members to achieve their unique and highest potential.

Avoiders create Lost Families.

Acceptors create Limited Families.

Anticipators create Legacy Families.

Your family is your legacy.

Will you leave a Lost, Limited or Legacy Family?

Your Next Right Step: Make a Decision

*It doesn't matter where you start.
It only matters where you end.*

Whether you begin as an Avoider or Acceptor, you have the ability to become an Anticipator. If you are already an Anticipator, you are typically open to the ideas this book provides to inspire your journey forward.

85% of families will suffer from the Cur$e, because family founders are unaware of this critical missing estate planning tool that will protect their family.

Please, don't let this be your family. Statistics are misleading. The reality is, it's all or nothing. Either your family remains intact, or the family unity is destroyed. It's 100% one way or the other. Odds are stacked against families who don't have a Legacy Family Plan. Without it, your family has an 85% chance of being 100% destroyed. That isn't what I want for you or your family, but it isn't up to me.

The decision is yours to make. Here's the good news and bad news. The good news is that you have total control of moving up the pyramid. The bad news is that you have total control of moving up the pyramid. The more effort you put into the process, the better the outcome you can expect for your family.

Are you ready

to become an Anticipator?

Now is your chance to become a part of the solution.

Legacy Family Planning is the proven system that, until now, has been the best kept secret of elite wealthy families. Blinded by the misconception that money is the key to their success, the real reason for their success was hiding in plain sight the entire time!

As the patriarch or matriarch of your family, you have the ability to radically and positively influence your family's future for generations to come. By implementing your own Legacy Family Plan, you protect your family from avoidable pain and suffering.

Even though it's your decision, you don't have to do it alone. Smart family leaders engage experienced professionals to guide them through the Legacy Family Planning Process.

You rely on professionals to draft your estate plan, invest your money and create your tax plan. Doesn't it make sense to add a Legacy Family Planning professional to your advisory team?

Our company's mission is to provide Legacy Family Planning education, training and support to financially successful families like yours. We've created books, manuals, webinars, workshops and retreats to help you and your family design your Legacy Family Plan.

Basic Components of Legacy Family Planning

The basic components of Legacy Family Planning include a series of documents created and adopted by family founders and the rising generation. Content for the documents is guided by a handful of values, the unifying family story, family mission statement, and the Basic Principles of Legacy Family Planning.

Most plans include a strategic plan, family constitution, stewardship plan, list of competencies and governance plan. Depending on your family assets, you may add shared asset plans and family bank documents to your plan. Together, these documents provide the framework to transfer your legacy to future generations.

Detailed instructions on how to create your Legacy Family Plan is the subject of my next soon to be released book, *The Legacy Family Way*. Meanwhile, we are constantly adding free resources to our website to assist you with your plan.

When you add Legacy Family Planning to your estate plan, you are protecting your family from being broke, bitter and blaming you. Your Legacy Family Plan will provide a firm foundation of values and character for generations to come. The intentional development of competencies in the four capital accounts of financial, social, intellectual and human will help your family achieve their highest potential.

But it isn't enough. Creating a legacy is a way of life. It takes more than a plan to create a legacy. It's when your day-to-day actions match the ideas identified in your plan, and you become a living example of your values, that your legacy is created.

The Basic Principles

The following basic principles are the foundation to build your Legacy Family Plan. Keep them in mind when you are creating your family's plan.

1. Your job is not your job. It's a vehicle to earn income. Your life is your job. Your job is to fully develop your unique potential and own your life.

2. Your family is your business. The purpose of your business is to fully develop each family member's unique potential and teach them to own their life.

3. A consciousness mindset is the key to success.

4. Each family member's authentic self is developed to realize his or her full potential. Inclusivity is the goal.

5. Provide opportunities for mistakes. Learning from experience builds self-confidence and self-esteem.

6. Provide opportunities to defer instant gratification. It is a critical component of long-term success.

7. Think like a coach to prevent judgment and build curiosity. When questions are asked instead of making assumptions, it reduces conflict.

8. Maximize time spent in Steven Covey's second quadrant of important but not urgent.

9. Everyone is doing their best.

10. The strength of the family is determined by its weakest relationship. Improving this relationship is top priority.

11. The family's success relies on creating a foundational attitude of gratitude. It is the antidote for entitlement.

12. Your values create the framework for decisions in accordance with the family mission statement.

13. Your family story creates a unified family culture.

14. Your mission statement provides clear guidance for investments in the four capital accounts.

15. There are four capital accounts to invest in, both personally, and as a family. The capital accounts include Financial, Intellectual, Social and Human Development.

16. Develop a list of competencies in the four capital accounts to provide a blueprint for a customizable educational plan.

17. Financial resources are invested to provide personalized competency training for family members.

18. Your formalized governance system provides the framework for making decisions.

19. Get help. Children are more apt to listen to a "professional" instead of a parent.

20. Be tenacious. Legacy Family Planning is a lifetime process that will have ups and downs. Focus on the positive results you are seeking.

The Benefits of Legacy Family Planning

Implementing Legacy Family Planning has transformed my life. Every day is an opportunity to create a legacy moment. Legacy moments are created by being consciously grateful **in the moment**. I feel fully alive when I am living legacy moments.

The more legacy moments you create, the more you want to create. Eventually, life becomes a string of legacy moments. Moments like releasing baby turtles in Cancun, or seeing my youngest granddaughter's eyes light up when I walk into a room, or enjoying the sunset with Gerald from the back porch of our Texas Hill Country ranch.

Creating legacy moments in difficult situations allows you to rise above petty issues. Visiting my brother in a federal prison is a daunting task. Each time I visit, the rules have changed, and I am surrounded by fellow visitors grumbling about those changes. Because visiting my brother is a legacy moment and I am grateful to see him. I am able to ignore the inconvenience of the changes and the grumblers that surround me.

Legacy moments are most powerful when created amidst difficult situations. By remaining consciously grateful in the moment, you access your ***best self***. Remember, your life is your job. By creating a legacy moment in a difficult situation, your best self is able to access your values. You not only set a positive example for your family, honestly, life is much more enjoyable.

Historically, few families have become Legacy Families. The ones who were able to achieve this status embraced the best kept secret hiding in plain sight. But not anymore.

Now it's your turn.

You now know what the real problem is and why it's important to create a Legacy Family Plan for your family. You know it's not the amount of wealth that matters, it's your courage to face your mortality, prepare your heirs, and build communication and trust. You have seen your legacy through their eyes and you know what you need to do to prepare them.

Remember the Epitaph from the Westminster Abbey Tomb?

. . . And now, as I lie on my deathbed, I suddenly realize: If I had only changed myself first, then by example I would have changed my family. From their inspiration and encouragement, I would then have been able to better my country and who knows, I may have changed the world.

What will you change for the sake of your family?

About the Author

CINDY ARLEDGE, MBA is an author, speaker, trusted family advisor and leader of the Legacy Family Revolution. She specializes in preparing heirs for entrepreneurial and financially successful families by supporting them in the creation and implementation of their Legacy Family Plan. After surviving the destruction of her own family following her parents' deaths, Cindy vowed to help other families avoid common pitfalls that plague the majority of wealth transfer events.

In her quest to protect her children and grandchildren, she discovered a secret process, used by elite ultra-wealthy families, known as Legacy Families. Combining her personal experience, decades of research, and her GRIPP Life™ Formula for Living, Cindy created her revolutionary signature program, and became her first case study.

Cindy's dedication to her process is extraordinary. Prior to sharing her GRIPP Life™ Formula for Living, Cindy set out to test her theory by walking the Camino de Santiago, a 500-mile pilgrimage across northern Spain with Ease and Grace. After successfully completing the journey, she penned her memoir, *My Camino, My Life*.

Her Vision as the Leader of the Legacy Family Revolution is to inspire 1,000,000 families to create their Legacy Family Plan. An active philanthropist, Cindy helped raise over $3 million dollars to build a women's shelter in Boerne, TX.

Cindy divides her time between her Texas Hill Country ranch that she enjoys with her husband and her "crazy grandma" house in north Texas where she goes to play with her four grandchildren.

Please join the Revolution Now!

Website: www.LegacyFamilyRevolution.com

Facebook: www.Facebook.com/LegacyFamilyRevolution

LinkedIn: www.LinkedIn.com/in/cindyarledge

Amazon Author Page: www.Amazon.com/author/cindyarledge

About the Illustrator

LISA ROTHSTEIN is the award-winning Madison Avenue ad agency copywriter and creative director best known for creating the famous "Wait'll We Get Our Hanes on You" campaign that changed America's underwear.

In her own creative consulting business, she uses a combo of cartooning and cutting-edge marketing strategy and language to help companies and entrepreneurs see their ideal clients and present their products, brand and message in a new and unforgettable way. She has both authored and illustrated Amazon best sellers in the business space. For creative consulting or cartoon projects: www. lisarothstein.com/cartoons

Additional Resources

Any project is harder when you don't have the right tools. **The Legacy Family Planning Toolkit** enables you to create your basic Legacy Family Plan via a simple step-by-step process.

This universal system is for matriarchs, patriarchs, widows/widowers, traditional families, newlyweds, single parents, blended families and any other familial unit on the planet. If your goal is to enjoy each day as a gift, protect your family from unnecessary avoidable pain and suffering, or create a legacy for future generations, you will love this toolkit.

What is the "Legacy Family Planning Toolkit"?

The Legacy Family Planning Toolkit is the ultimate guide for transferring values, character, family history and assets so that your children, grandchildren and unborn future family members will bless your memory and the contribution you made to their lives.

The Legacy Family Planning Toolkit provides **a fill-in-the-blank guide** to create your initial Legacy Family Plan, including assessments and powerful questions to guide you through the process.

Visit **www.LegacyFamilyRevolution.com**
for your free toolkit.

Special Book Bonus

These bonus pages are only available in the printed version of this book and have been added to provide you with a quick start to your Legacy Family Plan. To get the most from this bonus section, find a quiet place preferably in nature, to reflect on the questions posed. If you don't have access to nature, perhaps you can find a window with a view to inspire the answers you seek. They are inside, waiting to be revealed.

List the members of your family here:

_____

_____

_____

_____

_____

_____

_____

Applying the Basic Principles to You and Your Family

As you review this bonus section, while ideas are fresh in your mind, use a journal to capture your thoughts. I have included a copy of my family's draft Capital Competency List for your consideration. None of the principles are written in stone; please edit, add or delete, as needed, to create a list of Basic Principles and competencies your family can embrace.

1. *Your job is not your job. It's a vehicle to earn income. Your life is your job. Your job is to fully develop your unique potential and own your life.*

How are you developing your unique potential? Do you own your life, or does your life seem to own you? What is the single most important change you can make to improve your life?

2. *Your family is your business. The purpose of your business is to fully develop each family member's unique potential and teach them to own their life.*

How are you developing each family member's unique potential? Do they own their life, or are they trying to live up to expectations set by others? What one change can YOU make to help your family own their life?

3. *A consciousness mindset is the key to success.*

How do you define consciousness? How do you practice consciousness in your daily life?

4. *Each family member's authentic self is developed to realize his or her full potential. Inclusivity is the goal.*

How are family members encouraged to develop their authentic self? Are there any barriers to expressing their uniqueness?

5. *Provide opportunities for mistakes. Learning from experience builds self-confidence and self-esteem.*

Are mistakes used as learning opportunities? How can mistakes be used to build self-confidence and self-esteem?

6. *Provide opportunities to defer instant gratification. It is a critical component of long-term success.*

What techniques do you use to delay gratification? How are you teaching this concept to your family?

7. *Think like a coach to prevent judgment and build curiosity. When questions are asked instead of making assumptions, it reduces conflict.*

When communicating with your family, what is your tendency? Do you make assumptions, or ask questions? What is the single most important change YOU can make to improve communication with your family?

8. *Maximize time spent in Steven Covey's second quadrant of important but not urgent.*

Expressed as a percentage, how much time do you spend in the following quadrants?

important and urgent _____%
important and not urgent _____%
non-important and urgent _____%
non-important and not urgent _____%

9. *Everyone is doing their best.*

How you answer this question has been found to affect your belief about others. If you have trouble seeing yourself and others as doing their best, please read Brené Brown's groundbreaking book, *Rising Strong*.

10. *The strength of the family is determined by its weakest relationship. Improving this relationship is top priority.*

Your family is only as strong as its weakest member. Review your family member list and determine the weakest relationships. It could be any relationship: sibling, parent-child, husband-wife, or any other combination. Does anyone in your family suffer from abuse, addiction or untreated health issues? Ignoring these problems will not make them go away. Successful families do not try to tackle these challenges on their own, they employ help from professionals.

11. *The family's success relies on creating a foundational attitude of gratitude. It is the antidote for entitlement.*

Do family members feel entitled or grateful? How is gratitude practiced in your family?

12. *Your values create the framework for decisions in accordance with the family mission statement.*

What do you value and how do you share them with your family? Naming a handful of values provides the guidance system for creating a meaningful Legacy Family Plan. In our workshops and retreats, we assist family leaders in narrowing down the list to create the framework they need to identify their unique family story, mission statement and stewardship plan.

13. *Your family story creates a unified family culture.*

What family story best exemplifies your values? If you have difficulty finding a story, or deciding which one is best, host a relaxed family meal and reminisce about good times, and hard times. After choosing your story, create a three-to-five-word statement that will be easy for future generations to remember. Examples include, "Red's got it." and "Five dollars in his pocket."

14. *Your mission statement provides clear guidance for investments in the four capital accounts.*

Now that you have your top values identified, it's time to create a mission statement. What is your mission statement?

15. *There are four capital accounts to invest in, both personally, and as a family. The capital accounts include Financial, Intellectual, Social and Human Development.*

16. *Develop a list of competencies in the four capital accounts to provide a blueprint for a customizable educational plan.*

Use the sample list from the next section to create your list of competencies. This checklist provides the blueprint to train family members to master the skills they need to embody family values and achieve the family mission statement. Although Gerald and I made the list, and we are the family founders, we discovered many areas to further our education.

17. *Financial resources are invested to provide personalized competency training for family members.*

Successful Legacy Families see themselves as stewards of their financial assets, not owners. They accept responsibility to invest, grow and protect financial resources for the family's future. Most importantly, they train future generations to do the same, thereby growing the financial assets for an expanding number of family members. Do you consider yourself a steward of your resources? How are you teaching future generations to become stewards?

18. *Your formalized governance system provides the framework for making decisions.*

After you are gone, how will family members make decisions? Who will be allowed to vote, and under what circumstances?

19. *Get help. Children are more apt to listen to a "professional" instead of a parent.*

Successful families hire professionals to train their rising generation and create a "Board of Directors"

(BOD). The BOD and the entire family meets on a regular basis to build relationships with the family founders and the rising generation. Legacy Family leaders have the courage to ask, "Is this the best person to assist my family after I am gone?" Who will be on your BOD?

20. *Be tenacious. Legacy Family Planning is a lifetime process that will have ups and downs. Focus on the positive results you are seeking.*

When you hit a bump in the road of life, and your adopted basic principles don't provide you with the tools you need to thrive, create a new principle.

Sample Financial Capital Account Competency List

__ Do you have a healthy relationship with money?

__ Can you feel prosperous at any level of financial success?

__ Does your career choice support your family's wellbeing?

__ Are you supporting your lifestyle without help from others?

__ Have you determined how much is enough?

__ Have you created a Stewardship Plan?

__ Have you created a structured education plan for future generations?

Sample Social Capital Account Competency List

___ What aspect of life are you most passionate about improving?

___ What is your criteria for contributing time, talent and/or treasure?

___ How will you measure success for your contribution?

___ Have you created a structured education plan for future generations?

Sample Intellectual Capital Account Competency List

__ What is your formal education goal?

__ What areas of focus will you add to your life-long-learner education goal?

__ How will you achieve your education?

__ What is your dominant learning style?

__ Does your career choice satisfy you?

__ Are you supported by a coaching and/or mentoring relationship?

__ Have you created a structured education plan for future generations?

Sample Human Capital Account Competency List

___ Are you living an authentic life? (Congruent with your core motivation, values, personality, purpose, mission and Faith?)

___ Does your calendar and checkbook match your values?

___ Is your life balanced? Play, work, relationships, intellectual, health and spiritual?

___ Do you accept 100% responsibility for your life and encourage others to do the same?

___ Are you able to embrace challenges, heartaches and disappointments as opportunities?

___ Have you developed a formula for living that you use to provide guidance, direction and Faith?

___ Do you believe people, including yourself, are doing the best they can, given their current situation?

___ Do you have a personal mission statement?

___ Are you proficient in setting healthy boundaries?

___ Can you state what you need and ask for help?

___ Can you communicate effectively, participate in difficult conversations, and disagree with others without getting angry?

___ Do you put relationships with others before "being right"?

___ Do you listen for the meaning behind the words and actions?

___ Are you willing and able to be vulnerable?

___ Do you know how to be empathetic?

___ Have you identified your beliefs about entitlement?

___ Do you have a strong work ethic?

___ Do you know your Emotional Intelligence Score?

___ Do you have a plan in place to improve your

Emotional Intelligence Score?

___ Are you supported by a coaching or mentoring relationship?

___ Have you created a structured education plan for future generations?

Online Resources

The following assessments will help you discover
who you are at a deeper level.

Discover your core motivation and how to recognize
others' core motivations at:

www.colorcode.com

Discover your top-five strengths at:

www.strengthsfinder.com

Discover your personality traits at:

www.16personalities.com

Need some help with a tough conversation? Check
out the resources at:

www.deathoverdinner.org

Need help having a conversation about death and
end-of-life care decisions? Check out the resources at:

www.theconversationproject.org

What's on the Bookshelf?

Legacy Building

Willing Wisdom: 7 Questions to Ask Before You Die - Thomas William Deans, Ph.D.

Every Family's Business: 12 Common Sense Questions to Protect Your Wealth - Thomas William Deans, Ph.D.

Charity Case: How the Nonprofit Community Can Stand Up for Itself and Really Change the World - Dan Pallotta

When Helping Hurts: How to Alleviate Poverty Without Hurting the Poor and Yourself - Brian Fikkert and Steve Corbett

Family Wealth - Keeping It in the Family - James E. Hughes Jr.

The Legacy Family: The Definitive Guide to Creating a Successful Multigenerational Family - Lee Hausner and Douglas K. Freeman

Preparing Heirs: Five Steps to a Successful Transition of Family Wealth and Values - Roy Williams & Vic Preisser

The Voice of the Rising Generation - James E Hughes, Jr., Susan E. Massenzio, & Keith Whitaker

Intentional Wealth: How Families Build Legacies of

Stewardship and Financial Health - Courtney Pullen

Navigating the Dark Side of Wealth: A Life Guide for Inheritors - Thayer Cheatham Willis

Family Fortunes: How to Build Family Wealth and Hold on to It for 100 years - Bill Bonner and Will Bonner

Self-Discovery

The Prosperous Heart - Julia Cameron

The Artist's Way - Julia Cameron

Nonviolent Communication: A Language of Life - Marshall B. Rosenberg

The Gifts of Imperfection: Let Go of Who You Think You're Supposed to Be and Embrace Who You Are - Brené Brown

Loving What Is - Bryon Katie

Adulting: How to Become a Grown-up in 468 Easy(ish) Steps - Kelly Williams Brown

Radical Forgiveness - Colin Tipping

The Life-Changing Magic of Tidying Up - Marie Kondo

The Four Agreements - Don Miguel Ruiz

The Happiness Project - Gretchen Rubin

The Miracle Morning - Hal Elrod

The Conscious Parent: Transforming Ourselves, Empowering Our Children - Dr. Shefali Tsabary

The Introvert Advantage: How Quiet People Can Thrive in an Extrovert World - Marti Olsen Laney, Psy.D.

Outliers - Malcolm Gladwell

The Heart of the Soul - Gary Zukav

The Power of Now - Eckhart Tolle

Turning Hurts into Halos - Robert H. Schuller

Sacred Contracts - Caroline Myss

The Untethered Soul: The Journey Beyond Yourself - Michael A. Singer

Satan: An Autobiography - Yehuda Berg

The Laws of Spirit - Dan Millman

Aging and Death

The Conversation - Angelo E Volandes, M.D.

Learning to Speak Alzheimer's: A Groundbreaking Approach for Everyone Dealing with the Disease - Joanne Koenig Coste

Final Gifts: Understanding the Special Awareness, Needs and Communications of the Dying - Maggie Callanan and Patricia Kelley

When Roles Reverse - Jim Comer

On Death and Dying: What the Dying Have to Teach Doctors, Nurses, Clergy and Their Own Families - Elisabeth Kübler-Ross, M.D. and Ira Byock, M.D.

Answers About the Afterlife - Bob Olson

90 Minutes in Heaven - Don Piper

Losing Your Parents: Finding Yourself - Victoria Secunda

Other Impactful Books, Authors and Online Resources

The Diving Bell and the Butterfly - Jean-Dominique Bauby

The Shack - William P. Young

The Last Lecture - Randy Pausch

Simple Truths: Clear and Gentle Guidance on the Big Issues in Life - Kent Nerburn

Jim Stovall

Andy Andrews

John P. Strelecky

Mitch Albom

Robert Fulghum

Hire a Certified
Legacy Family Planner
to Speak at Your Event!

Are you looking for an attention-grabbing keynote speaker who will deliver a fresh new idea with a powerful message that adds to the long-term life success of your people?

Legacy Family Planning is the best kept secret used by elite families who want to transfer values, character and wealth to future generations without the drama. Staggering to consider that, on average, more than half of your audience doesn't even have a Last Will & Testament.

Contact our office to book a Certified Legacy Family Speaker as your keynoter and you're not only securing a profoundly impactful part of your program, you're investing in the long-term success of your people and their family's futures.

For more info, visit
www.LegacyFamilyRevolution.com
or call +1 (210) 414-7522 today.

NEED AN ATTORNEY FOR YOUR WILL OR OTHER FAMILY DOCUMENTS? YET DON'T KNOW HOW TO FIND THE BEST ONE FOR YOU?

LAWYER UP – THE SMART WAY is your guide to:

- Better understanding the strange breed known as "attorney"
- Finding the right lawyer for you
- "Checking out" that lawyer before committing
- Asking good questions
- Effectively managing the attorney's efforts on your behalf
- Mitigating legal fees
- Laughing along the way

Order ***LAWYER UP – THE SMART WAY***

at Amazon

or call +1 (210) 414-7522 today.

Motivate and
Inspire Others

Share a printed copy of this book.

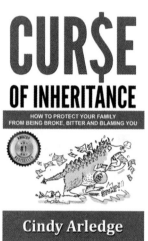

Retail: $20.00

Special Quantity Discounts

5 – 20 books	$17.50
21 – 99 Books	$ 9.95
100 + Books	$ 6.50

To place an order, contact:

210-414-7522

www.LegacyFamilyRevolution.com

info@LegacyFamilyRevolution.com

FAMILY RELATIONSHIPS $20.00

Most American families are unprepared for the greatest threat they have ever faced the Cur$e of Inheritance.

The Cur$e of Inheritance is an ugly monster of jealousy, fear and selfishness that crushes families, eats money and destroys lives. The Cur$e of Inheritance is born in an environment of loss and grief by unprepared heirs who feel entitled to unearned wealth, and tragically forget to see each other as human beings.

When Cindy Arledge's mom and dad passed away within eight months of each other, she was helpless to save the broken relationships created by her parent estate plan. Years later, after becoming a grandmother affectionately known as "Elmo", Cindy realized it was time to transform her tragedy into a solution protect her growing family's future and help other families do the same.

In this book you will discover the real reason why inheritances fail and the single most important change you can make to protect your family. Cindy shares secret planning tool wealthy families use to protect their families, provides the Legacy Family Planning basics, and a special bonus section that you can immediately implement for your family's benefit.

"A masterpiece that clearly defines wealth transfer conversations that families must have NOW to protect future relationships."
–Lauren Midgley, Time Behaviorist and author of
It's 6 a.m. and I'm Already Behind

"Hands down, Cindy Arledge has left no stone unturned in creating a lasting legacy. Want to set your family up for success? Pick up Cur$e of Inheritance"
–Kate Delaney, Business Motivational Speaker & NBC Talk Show

Legacy Inheritance Partners, Ltd

www.CindyArledge.com

www.LegacyFamilyRevolution.com

ISBN 978-0-9826953-

9 780982 695333